D0104871

DATE
DIFFERENT

A SHORT (BUT REAL) CONVERSATION ON
DATING, SEX, & MARRIAGE
FOR TEENAGERS (AND THEIR PARENTS)

GREG GIBSON

VERITAS PRESS 2015

Cover Design by Landon Reynolds

Layout & Design by Mathew B. Sims

www.MathewBryanSims.com

TO CORA
I WOULDN'T TRADE YOU
FOR ONE MILLION SONS.
WHEN IT'S TIME, MAY YOU
"DATE DIFFERENT" FOR THE
GLORY OF GOD

TABLE OF CONTENT

CHAPTER ONE
START HERE

A river flows downstream.

It all starts somewhere. It begins, flows downstream, and empties out into a final destination.

Much like a river, culture also flows downstream. Culture is created in bigger cities like New York, Los Angeles, Chicago, and Atlanta, and then it flows downstream into smaller cities, like Nashville and Memphis. Finally, culture flows over to my little city where I was born—Knoxville. And then even further into the town I currently live south of Knoxville—Maryville.

What's more, as culture flows downstream, it brings stuff with it. Much like a river, it brings the latest garbage, but for some reason, that garbage is what begins to define us. It's just weird like that.

In short, we are defined by the garbage from the river of culture.

It brings the coolest and latest fashion.

The coolest and latest music.

The coolest and latest movies.

The coolest and latest YouTube videos.

The coolest and latest social media whatever.

The coolest and latest view on something.

You got it... everything.

And because it brings everything, it also brings the way we view and practice dating, which is defined by the coolest and latest _____.

We watch movies that portray dating, sex, and marriage in a certain way, and so we think that is the way it is supposed to be. We listen to music that talks about guy/girl relationships in a certain way, and again, we think that is how it is to be.

Culture brings with it many things.

And one of those many things is how we *view* and *practice* dating, sex, and marriage.

Here is what I want to get off my chest right from the beginning: the way young people view and practice dating, sex, and marriage today = DISASTER!

I'll say it again.

The current approach to dating, sex, and marriage = **DISASTER**!

I'm not going to bore you with many statistics, but let me give you 3 that show us how disastrous it is.

FIRST STATISTIC: Nearly half (47%) of all high school students report having had sexual intercourse in 2011, a decline from 54% in 1991. Furthermore, males are slightly more likely than females to report having had sex (49% vs. 46%).

SECOND STATISTIC: 26% of female teens and 29% of male teens had more than one sexual partner in their lives. The percentage of high school students who report having had four or more sexual partners declined from 18% in 1995 to 15% in 2011.

THIRD STATISTIC: "Sexting" is the exchange of explicit sexual messages or images by someone's cell phone. 13% of 14–24 year olds report having shared a naked photo or video of themselves via digital communication such as the Internet or text messaging.[1]

Wow!

From these three statistics—and many, many, many more out there, as well as witnessing the after shocks of these statistics take place first hand working with teenagers and families for the last ten years—there has to be a better way to view and practice dating, sex, and marriage today.

I want to stay away from a few things throughout this book, however. First of all, I don't want this book to be anywhere close to the don't-have-sex-because-you-will-get-STDs chant, or the don't-have-sex-because-you-might-have-a-baby-out-of-wedlock chant, or even the don't-have-sex-because-it-will-make-you-feel-guilty-and-your-bab y-will-probably-be-ugly chant.

---

1 All 3 statistics come from the Kaiser Family Foundation (March 2013). http://www.kff.org/womenshealth/upload/3040-06.pdf

I also want to stay far away from the chants that say dating and sex are intrinsically bad, because they're not. Dating is good. Sex is good. I mean, really, it's good. *It's number one.* However, they are good only within the proper context wherein they were created by God to be enjoyed. We'll talk about this context as we go, but I want you to see right from the beginning these things are good. Very good!

Dating, sex, and marriage are all good things.

And, finally, I want to stay far away from the approach that is going to make you feel guilty over all, or make you think following Jesus is a list of do's and don'ts, or make you want to put a promise ring on the ring finger of your left hand when you finish reading this book. Not that there is anything wrong with a promise ring, but I'm not going to tell you to do that here.

This short book is about loving Jesus first and foremost. It's about pursuing him. Loving him. Chasing after him. Cherishing him. Finding him. Elevating him. Sprinting towards him. And then learning there has to be a different *view* and *practice* to this dating, sex, and marriage stuff.

JESUS IS GREATER THAN EVERYTHING

- Jesus > everything
- Jesus > dating
- Jesus > sex

- Jesus > orgasms
- Jesus > marriage
- Jesus > singleness
- And even...
- Jesus > a life of one night stands
- Jesus > porn
- Jesus > messing around
- Jesus > your dream girl or guy
- Jesus > _____ *(fill in the blank)*

Yes, it is about seeing dating, sex, and marriage in a different light, but you can't change your view on these things unless you change your view on Jesus. It's all about a life-long pursuit of God. This God who emptied himself, who, though he was in the form of God, did not count equality with God a thing to be grasped, but made himself nothing, taking the form of a servant, being born in the likeness of men. And being found in human form, he humbled himself by becoming obedient to the point of death, even death on a cross (Phil. 2:11).

Therefore, because of Jesus, I think it is worth our time to re-examine everything, especially what I think is killing our current and up-and-coming generations... which is our current *view* and *practice* of dating, sex, and marriage.

And if Jesus is greater than everything, then Jesus changes everything.

Again, Jesus changes everything.

I can't say it enough—Jesus changes EVERYTHING! Literally everything!

Even how we *view* and *practice* dating, sex, and marriage.

If this is true, then let's change the way we date, pursue relationships, and pursue marriage.

WHO IS EVEN TALKING ABOUT THIS STUFF?

Magnifying glasses are great for seeing things... if you're somewhat blind.

But when it comes to the dating culture of teenagers, and the up-and-coming generations, you don't really need one to see how absolutely terrible it is. The statistics speak for themselves. It's horrible.

The problem seems, to me, as big as an elephant. So, where do we even begin at tackling such a culturally defined *view* and *pursuit*? That's the question right there.

Everywhere I go people are asking this question. Everywhere I go, people are talking about this. When I read Christian blogs and articles, people are talking about this. When I write my own blogs, I find myself talking about this more often than not. Seriously, everyone is talking about this, but there are 3 major groups of people who seem like they are talking about this dating-sex-marriage-thing more than anyone else. And they are:

#1 PARENTS

Almost 100% of the time, when a parent comes to talk to me about their son or daughter, it is about dating, sex, or marriage. Parents of teenagers aren't really talking about marriage yet, because it makes them want to pee their pants, but they do want advice on the dating and sex part.

I have had parents tell me I have free reign to talk to their kids about sex in my messages at our student ministry services (and that's anything and everything about sex). I have also had parents approach me to give the "sex talk" to their kids for them, because they don't know how to do it, and they think it would be more beneficial coming from me—for some odd reason—like I'm the designated "sex talk" guy or something.

Parents are always asking, "Can I get advice for my son/daughter in this dating relationship?" My next question is always the same:

Well, mom and dad, have you set standards for what dating will look like for your son or daughter?

The answer is almost always a resilient **NO**. They have simply decided to tackle the issues and headaches when they arise, instead of talking through the issues with their child, setting a standard for what dating will look like for them, and then shepherding their heart to practice manhood and womanhood and pursue dating and marriage in a healthy way. And at this point, they are pretty much holding on for dear life.

What I think we should do is pretty simple.

FIRST: We need to begin teaching our children at an early age about dating, sex, and marriage.

SECOND: We need to prepare them for marriage at an early age (we'll talk about that as we go on, too).

THIRD: We need to put a standard in place for what dating is going to look like in our homes—a standard they can take with them when they leave. A standard that is grace-centered, Christ-centered, and extremely intentional.

#2 STUDENT PASTORS

It seems like I am always talking to student pastors about the tensions of dating, sex, and marriage. They are asking questions like:

- What do you do when you have middle school students who are dating?
- What do you do when you have high school students in a sexual relationship?
- What do you do when you are teaching that dating is intended for marriage, but parents don't seem to care and don't back your position/teaching?

Student pastors are beside themselves on this issue.

#3 TEENAGERS

Man, this is all teenagers want to talk about. This is the number one question I get from students. And on the other side of the coin, this is also the number one source of drama and gossip I had to deal with in student ministry.

I'm not trying to be crude, but I overhear teenage boys play the, "Who would you rather have sex with?" game every time I walk into a public high school. It's pretty sickening.

I overhear teenage girls gossip about the boy they like but so-and-so also likes him, and my wife seems to be counseling young ladies often about their recent mishap with their newest boy-friend.

Again, it's sickening, but it's also very sad.

Have you counseled someone who has said these things lately? Maybe you are the one saying these things:

- "So-and-so broke up with me and I don't know what to do."
- "I can't be in leadership anymore, because I've been having sex."
- "I like this person... what should I do about it?"
- "I'm struggling with looking at porn."

Have you seen the passive-aggressive Facebook posts about recent fights or breakups? I'm sure you have. Again, maybe I'm talking about you.

Christian kids from Christian homes with no con-cept of true manhood and womanhood, and no standard of dating from their parents, are accept-ing the current way of dating.

GOD, ME, THEM, US, WE

Whenever I talk with students, parents, or pastors—or those who work with these groups—I always talk about this topic with 5 words as my guide: God, Me, Them, Us, We

These five words are not only the foundation of my conversation with teenagers and parents, but also the pillars of this short book. I've tried to take all of this content and sum it up in a way that is memorable—in a way where both teenagers and parents can have a roadmap, as it were, to guide them through these ever important years.

Here's what I mean by these 5 words:

GOD: In all things, we must begin with God. God created all things and gave everything a design and purpose—even dating, sex, and marriage. We must learn what these purposes are and then lean into these purposes according to how God designed us to live.

ME: After our conversation on God and his design for dating, sex, and marriage, we focus on ourselves. The teenage years, I believe, are a season to prepare for marriage, not a season to practice dating. What does it mean to prepare yourself for marriage during this season of your life?

THEM: It takes two to be in a relationship, right? But most of the time, we get it all wrong when it comes to the "other person" in the relationship. As we are moving into the stages of a relationship, we often find ourselves focusing more on *attraction* than *character*. During this chapter, we'll work through some green light and red light questions to see if we should move forward with a potential relationship.

US: If you are currently in a relationship, there should be a standard according to which you should date. This standard is the Lord Jesus Christ, but the application from your relationship with Christ, and the truth that Jesus changes everything, should lead you to date different. We'll also have a frank discussion on sex during this chapter.

WE: This last word—we—brings the Christian community and our families into the mix. As Christians, it is important to have others involved in our lives. We need older men to mentor and disciple younger men, and vice-versa for the ladies. We've created a culture where parents aren't involved in their children's relationships. We throw around words like *privacy* and *legalism* and think it's somehow better for them to figure it out on their own—to make their own mistakes. When we do this, we set them up for failure in their current relationships, as well as their potential future relationships. Bringing others into our relationships is the foundational principle for what it means to date different.

THE COLOR PURPLE

So, how do we tackle this massive purple elephant?

One bite at a time.

CHAPTER ONE: START HERE

We tackle this disaster with one mom and dad at a time that will put standards in their home and point their kids toward Jesus and a healthy way of dating. **We tackle this disaster with one young person at a time that will pursue Jesus above everything else.** We tackle this disaster with one student pastor at a time that will keep pressing on, not giving up, even if it seems no one is with him yet.

Dads, moms, student pastors, and young people must all change their view of dating.

It has to change. That's for sure. It can't stay the same. It just can't.

So, I challenge you: let's change it together. Right now. What say you?

Good.

Purple is the color made when pink (or red—but pink for our purposes) and blue come together. It's a girly color, in my humble opinion. It has been said to symbolize things like purity, good judgment, magic, mystery, as well as royalty. For our purposes here, though, purple will symbolize the pursuit of oneness. Yes, I am walking on a thin line of cheese-balls even talking about an age-old student ministry joke. I know that.

Maybe you've heard it said this way, "When pink and blue come together, it makes purple. No purpling in this ministry."

Well, I want to redeem everything about this topic—even the cheesy stuff. Let's begin our conversation with God.

CHAPTER TWO
GOD>ME>THEM>US>WE

**In all things, begin with God
and his design for it.**

In all things, we must begin with God. All too often, we begin with the thing we are discussing. For instance, if we are discussing why sex is gross or good (which we will discuss), the discussion often begins with the act of sex itself, then making its way to the person's experiences—good or bad—with sex. This is backwards.

We must begin with God.

Hebrews 11:1-3, for me, is really the precursor to this conversation. It reads:

> Now faith is the assurance of things hoped for, the conviction of things not seen. **2** For by it the people of old received their commendation. **3** By faith we understand that the universe was created by the word of God, so that what is seen was not made out of things that are visible.

The author of Hebrews begins with a word that stands above all other words in our discussions on the things of God. That word is *faith*. We see that *faith* is the assurance of things hoped for, the conviction of things not seen. We begin our conversation with God, because as Christians we believe God is actually there, and he created all things.

Faith is trust—trust that God is actually there, even though we can't see him.

Therefore, by faith (the conviction of things not seen), we believe God spoke the world into existence. Not only that, but we believe he spoke the world into existence out of nothing. He didn't have a ball of play-doh just sitting around bored out of his mind making play-doh snakes, and then decide to make the universe out of it. No way. He made everything out of nothing. And he gave everything a purpose and everything a form and shape.

By faith, we believe God is actually there, created the world, and created the things of this world.

GOD CREATED MARRIAGE FOR HIS GLORY AND OUR GOOD

All the way back in the book Genesis, after God created the world, he created marriage. In fact, before government, before nations, before languages, and before the church, God created the institution of marriage. It was to be the foundation of the progress and flourishing of humanity. In Genesis 2:18-25, the Bible records God creating marriage in this way:

> Then the Lord God said, "It is not good that the man should be alone; I will make him a helper fit for him." **19** Now out of the ground the Lord God had formed every beast of the field and every bird of the heavens and brought them to the man to see what he would call them. And whatever the man called every living creature, that was its name. **20** The man gave names to all livestock and to the birds of the heavens and to every beast of the field. But for Adam there was not found a helper fit for him. **21** So the Lord God caused a deep sleep to fall upon the man, and while he slept took one of his ribs and closed up its place with flesh. **22** And the rib that the Lord God had taken from the man he made into a woman and brought her to the man. **23** Then the man said,
>
> > "This at last is bone of my bones
> > and flesh of my flesh;
> > she shall be called Woman,
> > because she was taken out of Man."
>
> **24** Therefore a man shall leave his father and his mother and hold fast to his wife, and they shall become one flesh. **25** And the man and his wife were both naked and were not ashamed.

Here a few things I want you to see about the awesomeness of marriage.

1. GOD CREATED MARRIAGE; THEREFORE, IT IS **GOOD**!

Everything about marriage is good. Do you know that? Remember in chapter one, we talked about how garbage flows downstream in rivers, and how the culture river brings filth and garbage downstream to us? Well, as we have stated, a bad view and pursuit of marriage is one of those things.

Culture will tell you marriage is bad. Culture will tell you marriage is a boulder that weighs you down. Culture will tell you to go and live your life to the fullest, and then after you have done everything you want to do, after you travel to all the places you want to go, only then can you settle down and get married.

But here's what I want you to see: God created marriage, and it is GOOD!

In fact, it is so good that God created it before he created any other thing for man. When God created Adam, he told him to go out and begin naming animals—dog, cat, donkey, blue-footed booby. Everything had a second pair but Adam, and God new it wasn't good for Adam just to wonder around in the Garden by himself. Imagine how lame that would have been? Instead, God knocked Adam out, took one of his ribs, and formed the woman out of him. It was golden! Adam awoke and then gloriously shouted some of my favorite words in all of Scripture, "This at last," he said.

The woman whom God created for Adam was good. "This at last," Adam joyously proclaimed. It's almost as if Adam was hit with his first case of hormones as he saw the beautiful naked body of Eve standing before him.

God created man and woman, he put them in the Garden of Eden together, and they were both naked. The best part about this was they were also unashamed. Sin had yet to enter the world. The man and the woman were naked together in the Garden; it was glorious, and it was also good.

2. IN MARRIAGE, A MAN **LEAVES** HIS FAMILY AND MAKES A **NEW FAMILY** WITH HIS WIFE.

When a man and wife join in marriage, the Bible says a man leaves his father and mother and holds fast to his wife. This is what is known as leaving and cleaving. You leave your father and mother and cleave to your spouse. In doing so, you become ONE. You must prepare you children to leave one day. If you are dating or engaged, then you are TWO. You are not ONE... yet. If you are single, then you still have to find that TWO before you can even think about becoming ONE.

Do you get it?

This is a daunting thing, yes, but it is a good thing. Let me ask you this: As a teenager, how are you preparing yourself to leave home one day?

How are you preparing yourself to make a new family one day?

Are you rolling up your sleeves, working hard, learning God's Word, and preparing yourself to leave your home and create a new family? Do you even take showers on a regular basis? Maybe you should start there.

Before we end this point, though, I think it would be beneficial to have a quick conversation on the current culture of parenting teenagers. Often times, at least in my experience, the majority of teenagers graduate high school and stay as close to home as possible. After graduation, they either go to a college or university that is close to home, or stay home for a season and work odd jobs here and there.

The point I want to tackle is that this type of thinking bleeds into more than just the college years of teenagers, twenty-somethings, and their parents. After graduation, college graduates try to find a job in their home community or city, staying close to their parents, even potentially delaying the marks of adulthood. This makes the leaving and cleaving process much more difficult. There are many implications we could discuss here about why this is important, but we must begin to prepare our teenagers to actually leave home when they become adults, if for no other reason than to cleave to his or her spouse.

3. ADAM WAS NAKED WITH HIS WIFE.

Adam and his wife, Eve, were naked and not ashamed. Here's what I want you to see: Adam was only naked WITH HIS WIFE!

Not his girlfriend.

Not his fiancé.

Adam was naked with his wife. Because they were ONE!

Nakedness—and the lack of guilt in it—is found only in marriage, because this is how God designed it to be. When we find ourselves falling into sexual sin, we find that lots of guilt is attached to it. This guilt is alive in us because any sexual fulfillment outside of marriage is sin. It's not how God created it to be.

And you know what, being naked with your spouse is a good thing. It's not a gross thing. Furthermore, it's not the only thing we should desire in marriage. It is absolutely a gift from God, which we'll talk more about in the next chapter.

DO NOT AWAKEN LOVE UNTIL TWO BECOMES ONE

In the book of Song of Solomon, we see the most graphic depiction of the marriage bed in all of Scripture. In Song of Solomon 2:8, we read this:

I adjure you, O daughters of Jerusalem, by the gazelles or the does of the field, that you *not stir up or awaken love until it pleases.*

In other words, do not awaken love until everything that happens in Genesis 1-2 becomes a reality in your life. Do not awaken love until you are mature enough—you have prepared yourself—to pursue someone to be your spouse. Stay far away from it until then.

Do not awaken love until you are ready to leave your mom and dad's house and start a new family. Until then, you are just pretending... and probably sinning.

Do not awaken love until TWO becomes ONE.

The most obvious application here is sexual, but I also want you to see there are some implications for the emotional state of a relationship. Do you say, "I love you," to your boyfriend or girlfriend without any form of commitment attached to those words? If so, those words mean nothing, and at the same time, they mean everything. When you awaken love—sexual or emotional intimacy—then there should be a major form of commitment attached to that love.

The world in which sexual and emotional intimacy should live is marriage. Outside of this forever commitment, it means nothing. There are no strings attached. The damage, however, is devastating. When you awaken love before its time, then it leaves a devastating path of brokenness behind it.

SIDE NOTE: I wonder if parents actually think through the consequences of dating for young people where intimacy is awaken before it is ready. Parents often let their teenagers date, and by default are accepting the consequences.

Teens date >
No standard from dad/mom is given >
Accept the statistics, consequences, and potential disaster
=Path of devastating brokenness.

Here's the deal, the Bible calls marriage a reflection of Christ and His Bride (Eph. 5:22-33). That's a pretty big and incredible comparison, and if we are going to take this pursuit seriously, then how much greater should we pursue this *redeemed approach* to dating, sex, and marriage differently?

I want to put it this way for you as we move ahead: We can either ACCEPT the way things are, REJECT the way things are, or REDEEM (or change) the way things are in how we *view* and *practice* dating, sex, and marriage.

ACCEPT IT

Accepting it means we are fine with how things are, and we are not going to fight to change it. It's easier to not fight, for us to stay the way we are, and for things to stay the way they are.

This means a few things, however. It means that you:

1. ACCEPT THE STATISTICS.

It means you accept that your son or daughter could be 50% of the high school population that has sexual intercourse before they graduate high school.

It means you accept the statistic. At this point, it's as simple as a coin flip. This is unacceptable.

2. ACCEPT THE NORM.

It means you accept the way things are, and you are okay with fitting into the current view of dating, sex, and marriage in our culture. But if Jesus changes everything, then there is no possible way we can just sit there and be okay with the norm.

3. ACCEPT THE POSSIBILITIES.

It means you accept the possibilities. It means you accept the fact that your son or daughter might experience with sex in their teenage years. It means that you are okay with the possibilities of what could occur when your daughter is in a dark room, using one blanket, and laying horizontal on one couch with a hormone-crazed boy. And just so you know, it's not nothing. And if you believe that, then you're clueless.

It also means that you, as a teenager, are okay with the possible outcomes of a romantic and intimate relationship before it should be romantic and intimate.

And if Jesus changes everything, then there is not a possible way on this planet we can be okay with that. We, as followers of Jesus, should not also be followers of temptation.

4. ACCEPT THE DISASTER.

And it means you accept the disaster, because most of the time, there is one.

Again, if Jesus changes everything... well, you know the rest of the bit by now.

REJECT IT

Or we can reject it. We can reject the way dating is currently practiced, how sex is currently viewed, and how marriage is currently pursued. If we reject it, however, we find ourselves at the complete opposite end of the spectrum. This approach brings these things:

- Legalism.
- A bad or gross view of sex.
- The teaching that says: Do not have sex because it leads to guilt and sin, STDs, pregnancy, and feeling dirty.
- Arranged marriages.
- Purity commitments that are destined to be broken.
- Living on a compound and burning all of your secular music.

I don't think this is what we need to do either.

REDEEM IT

Who says we have to keep doing the same things the same way?

Especially if the current system is a disaster. What we want to do is redeem the way dating is currently practiced, and redeem how we teach, talk about, and view this whole dilemma of dating, sex, and marriage.

To redeem something simply means to reclaim ownership of something by paying a price for it.

Much like how Jesus *redeemed* us by paying the ultimate price for us, we need to redeem how we *view* and *practice* dating, sex, and marriage, by paying a price for it. He gave his life to redeem us. He paid the highest cost. He paid the ultimate price. We have to go against the trend, but that's not the only cost.

I say we stop swimming with the downstream current of the culture river, and begin attempting to swim upstream. Let's change the way we practice dating. Let's change the way we view sex. Let's change the way we pursue marriage. To change, however, means that things can't stay the way they are. I know that sounds like an obvious statement, but as you keep reading, and as you learn about some of the changes I am suggesting we make, you are probably going to disagree with them at first glance. But again, I will keep reminding you, if Jesus changes everything, then he changes everything... even how we do this dating, sex, and marriage thing.

Things have to change. They must.

We don't want to accept the way things are and keep sweeping the current approaches under the rug. We don't want to just reject the way things are, and wrap ourselves in bubble wrap and duck tape, or move to the middle of nowhere, or join an all guys school, or just put a promise ring on our finger. No. Those things are just behavior modifications that don't get to the root of the issues. We want to redeem it and change our thinking.

Here's what this means:

1. JESUS SAVES US.

When Jesus saves us, he saves us from sin and hell, but he also saves us into his family. This is called the gospel. The gospel is good news. Believe me, it's so good.

I have defined the gospel in my book, *Reformational Manhood*, as follows:

> The gospel is the message of God, man, sin, Christ, and response.
>
> What is more, the gospel is the message that God, the Father, created the world good, and created humans in his image as very good. Man was created to be in relationship with his Creator, and to give glory to him in all things. Early in the story, however, man

sinned by substituting himself for God, and all of creation was broken.

Sin separated man from God. The rest of the story finds man in turmoil with God and in need of a Savior to pay the punishment for sin that man deserves (again, this is the meaning of the word *redeem*). Man, however, could not pay his own debt. Jesus, God the Son, then came to earth and lived a perfect life—because we could not—and died on a cross as a substitute for sin.

In doing so, Jesus substituted himself for us, taking the punishment that we deserve—in the same way Adam substituted himself for God in the garden. Jesus arose from the dead, defeated death, and ascended into Heaven at the Father's right hand. After taking his rightful place, Jesus sent God, the Holy Spirit, to call people to salvation, redeem cities and cultures, and build his church until he comes back.

He is making all things new.

Jesus, through the Spirit, is calling everybody everywhere to repent of all sin and to put their faith in him for the forgiveness of sin. Jesus will return, but he will not return empty handed. He will bring the New Heavens and New Earth. He will return as a Warrior King—one who will completely defeat sin and death and usher in the completeness of *shalom* (peace).

He will then judge all people everywhere who have ever lived on earth, whether or not they have repented of sin and have put their faith in him. Jesus will then judge everybody who has ever lived. He will then graciously forgive those who do repent and punish those who do not by sending them to the real, eternal, and conscience torments of hell.

That is the gospel.[2]

It is also truth.

You see, the gospel is so much more than the story of Jesus. It is that, yes. But it is also the entire story of Scripture, unfolding to a specific goal, which is Jesus Christ's return. And the amazing thing here is that Jesus saves us into this story—this story, then, becomes our story.

2. JESUS CHANGES US.

When Jesus saves us, it doesn't stop there. After we are saved, we begin a process—a journey with him—called sanctification. In other words, we begin a journey with him to become more like him.

I heard my friend Alvin Reid say it like this one time, "We must rest in our salvation, but we must live and work in our sanctification."

---

2 Another great little book for understanding the gospel more is, *What is the Gospel?*, by Greg Gilbert.

Jesus changes both our hearts and our minds. Our hearts are pointed toward God in repentance and faith, and our minds also begin the process of being renewed.

The Apostle Paul mentions this in Romans 12:2, when he says this:

> Do not be conformed to this world, but be transformed by the *renewal of your mind,* that by testing you may discern what is the will of God, what is good and acceptable and perfect.

When Jesus saves us, he renews—or changes— our minds on things, which leads me to point 3.

3. JESUS CHANGES HOW WE VIEW AND **PRACTICE** THINGS.

You see, when Jesus saves us, he changes our thinking, and when he changes our thinking, then he changes our *views* on things. If we understand this, then our *practice* of dating, sex, and marriage simply cannot stay the same. The logic is pretty clear. Jesus saves us. Jesus changes us. Therefore, Jesus changes how we *view* and *practice* things.

Dating is one of those things.

Sex is one of those things.

Marriage is one of those things.

Let's talk about that now.

CHAPTER THREE
GOD>**ME**>THEM>US>WE

**ME: This is a season to prepare,
not a season to practice.**

After we begin with God, we must turn the magnifying glass to ourselves.

I hope it has been clear from the first two chapters that we must begin with God in everything. If we don't, then we do not have a foundation for which to make these types of truth claims about how we should live as Christians.

So, to recap, the river of culture brings the garbage of culture into our homes and lives. We often reflect the culture in our dating and relationships. I am claiming that Jesus changes everything—even how we view and practice dating, sex, and marriage as teenagers, and how we equip and prepare our children for the important institution of marriage as parents. To begin our discussion, we began with God. God created everything, and he gives purpose and order to everything. Let's now move the discussion to ourselves.

THIS IS YOUR SEASON

As a young person, this is your season. I think the Enemy, as well as our flesh, too often go to war on the security of who we are in Christ. If you are a Christian, then you have been bought by Jesus (1 Cor. 6:20). You are a new creation in Christ (2 Cor. 5:12); the old is gone and the newness of being redeemed by him has become a reality in your life.

The result of not leaning into this truth, and preaching this beloved gospel to yourself daily, is that your insecurities creep into who you are. As a teenager, you then begin to believe the lies that aren't true. You begin to believe lies like these:

- I am not good enough.
- I am not pretty enough.
- I am a failure.
- I am lonely and have no friends.
- I will never amount to anything.
- I have nasty back pimples.

And then instead of running to the Rock of Ages, you find yourself running to other people to give you comfort, security, and sanctuary about your insecurities. You, then, trade this *season of singleness* for a season of dating other people, often at the expense of what God could potentially be doing in you and through you. You find yourself running to other functional saviors.

My encouragement right from the beginning of this chapter is pretty simply—use your singleness well. Use your singleness for big things. See this season of your life not as a season to be tied emotionally to someone else, but see this season of your life as a blank canvas.

You can do anything you want to do in the world. You can play sports without distraction. You can travel without distraction. You can commit to serving in your local church, or other non-profit organizations in your community, without distraction.

My prayer is that you would embrace this reality in your life.

This is the greatest time of your life to take risks and be distraction free from potential relationships.

THIS IS YOUR SEASON!

Go overseas and do mission work for a few years. Travel. Use your summers to serve outside of your state—or country. Experience new cultures. Be bold and courageous for the King of the universe. But to do so, you must learn to *date different.*

THE SILENT KILLER OF FUNCTIONAL SAVIORS

I mentioned the word "functional savior" a few lines above. What I mean by this is simple. Instead of placing our worship, pursuits, and aims on Jesus, we replace him with other things that function as saviors.

CHAPTER THREE: ME

One of my favorite definitions of worship is by the next generation guru, Louie Giglio. He defines worship this way, saying, "Worship is our response to what we value the most."[3] I think he is exactly right. When we understand worship as a lifestyle, and not something we do only on Sunday mornings, then worship is a habitually constant response to something—whether that something is God or not.

When I was in high school, the 3 things I valued the most were basketball, popularity, and girls. I was the stereotypical normal teenager who struggled with trying to figure out life amidst all of the things youth culture throws at you as a young person. It wasn't until a couple of weeks after I graduated high school that I saw I had been worshipping the wrong saviors all along.

They were functional saviors. They took the place of the true Savior. I was still a worshipper, but I worshipped the wrong things—the things I valued the most.

This conversation becomes a reality in the lives of teenagers and parents, more than ever, when we talk about dating, sex, and marriage.

The first thing you need to do is evaluate. What are the functional saviors in your life? What are the things—or people—that have become the objects of your worship? When we do

---

3 Giglio, Louie. *The Air I Breathe: Worship as a Way of Life* (Sisters, Oregon: Multnomah Publishers, 2003), 10.

this, we can turn (repent) from these idols in our lives and move our worship back towards the King of the universe.

I see this more than ever with young girls. When dad, or a healthy male authority, isn't present in the home, young girls often find their identity and security in running towards boys. Daddy issues become masked in the unhealthy craving of relationships with boys.

Dads, we must work harder than ever at pursuing and dating our daughters.

PREPARE YOURSELF RIGHT NOW

This is a season to prepare, not a season to practice.

Today, teenagers practice dating like they are buying shoes. We try on one pair, walk around for a bit, look in the mirror, and do a couple of sprints around the store just to be safe. Or maybe that's just me.

Teenagers (and everyone, really) date just like that. Dating has become a recreational sport. In sports, you have to practice a ton to be good. For some reason, we have carried over that same mindset into dating.

We have replaced God with ourselves. We have replaced God's design for dating, sex, and marriage with our own desires for it.

We see dating and sex more as "something we do" instead of "something for which we prepare ourselves." Again, this is not a season to practice; this is a season to prepare for marriage. At first glance, that might sound a little weird. It might feel strange to tell your teenager dating is something you do later in life. That sounds a bit risky, right? A bit too legalistic? No way! In fact, I think it's pretty dang courageous to parent in this way. It's absolutely counter-cultural.

What if you told your friends you weren't dating right now because you are using this season of your life as a season of preparation? You are preparing to date later in life. What a statement!

With this understanding, and with all my chips on the table, here is what I mean by all of this:

YOU SHOULD DATE WHEN YOU ARE READY FOR MARRIAGE.

That is counter-cultural stuff right there. That is *dating different*. Parents, if you parent your teenagers to use their teenage years for preparing for marriage, that is *dating different*. Teenagers, if you use your teenage years to do big things, go to far places, and serve those who need it, that is *dating different*. Let's do this! I don't know if you're up for the challenge, but if you are, here are ways you can prepare yourself right now.

THOUGHTS FOR YOUNG MEN ON PREPARING FOR MARRIAGE

Again, if we are going to be risky and bold in our pursuit of King Jesus, then we must *date different*. Here are a few things I would suggest:

1. DON'T PURSUE GIRLS, PURSUE CHRIST, THEN PURSUE A WOMAN.

I want to raise the bar for young men. Instead of going from girl to girl, pursue Christ. Focus on having a growing and vibrant relationship with your Savior. Find your identity in Christ alone.

Rarely do guys pursue one girl in their teenage years and stay with the same girl until marriage. The reality is guys go from girl to girl to girl, not because of emotional feelings or "love," but for one reason only—sexual attraction. Once guys get what they want from girls, they begin to lose interest. I talk with young guys all of the time who are ending relationships because they aren't "interested anymore." When I ask them if they have been sexually active with their girlfriends, they squirm like a fish out of water, embarrassed to answer the question.

I know the truth, though. Guys pursue girls because of physical attraction. Instead, my challenge is to pursue Christ, and when you are ready, pursue a young woman who has been practicing something similar.

2. PREPARE YOURSELF FOR MARRIAGE BY PURSUING THE MARKS OF MANHOOD.

If you want something for which to aim (no pun intended), then aim for the marks of true manhood. In my book, *Reformational Manhood*, I have written to young men, pleading with them to pursue what I would call the marks of biblical manhood. Here are a few of them:

KNOWING THE GOSPEL

Begin by knowing the gospel. Don't just know it, though, know it enough to share it and teach it.

SACRIFICIAL LEADERSHIP

Read books on leadership. Get around men you respect, not just those who are funny. Get involved in different leadership opportunities in your church, school, and community. Understand, however, leadership is not dictator leadership—shouting orders at people because of your title or position. In Scripture, we find Jesus as the greatest leader of all time, and he led by serving. Leadership is sacrificial. It's giving up yourself for those you are leading. Work towards that end.

HARD WORK

This is one thing that will set you above others. If you are a young man who works hard, then people will notice. Develop this discipline at an early age. Work hard in school. Work hard at being the best son and brother you can be. Work hard at being the best friend you can be. Work hard at your job. One day, you will be called to provide for your family. Will you do whatever you have to do to make that happen?

PROTECTING WOMEN
AND CHILDREN AT ALL COSTS

I think this characteristic of manhood sets men apart from women distinctively. Notice I said set apart, not above. John Piper says it best when he poses the question, "Who gets in the lifeboat first when the ship is sinking?" God has called men to lay down their lives, if necessary, for women and children. This is what is known as the mark of protection. Begin to see yourself as a protector of women—in all areas. This means you protect women not just physically, but also emotionally and sexually. This is a great and honorable task. Are you ready to raise the bar here?

MAKING GOOD DECISIONS
FOR THE BENEFIT OF OTHERS

I place this as a mark of mature manhood, because men must learn to become good decision-makers. The opposite of a good decision-maker is someone who is passive. There is nothing worse than a passive-lazy man who refuses to do the hard work in making decisions. Become a confident decision-maker. If it proves to be a bad decision, don't go fetal position. Own up to your decision and fix it. However, don't be passive. And here is the kicker—become a decision-maker for others. Filter your decisions through questions like, "How does this effect other people, such as my family, friends, co-workers, etc.?"

3. INVITE OTHER DUDES INTO YOUR LIFE FOR **WISDOM** AND **ACCOUNTABILITY** (BOTH OLDER MEN AND PEERS).

Don't be a loan ranger. You will fail. Everyone needs to be accountable to someone. If you don't have accountability, then get it. When you have other dudes in your life, both the same age and older men, then you will have both accountability and mentorship happening. Sometimes young men need other men to challenge them in their spiritual walk, and sometimes they need men to show them how to shoot a gun. Men need wisdom and accountability from those who have gone before them.

4. PURSUE A GIRL WITH HER DAD'S APPROVAL, BUT DON'T DATE UNTIL YOU'RE **READY** FOR MARRIAGE.

I don't think I can say it enough. Date when you are ready for marriage. And when you are ready for marriage, make sure her father (or another male figure in her life) is involved. Until then, you are only a *potential*, bro. Don't act like anything but a *potential*. If you really want to be counter-cultural, when you are ready to pursue a dating relationship, then ask her dad for permission. This will set you apart, and prepare the way for a smoother foreseeable future.

THOUGHTS FOR YOUNG LADIES ON PREPARING FOR MARRIAGE

It might go without saying, but young ladies should adopt similar principles, as well. Here are a few I would suggest:

1. DON'T PURSUE BOYS, PURSUE CHRIST, AND A MAN WILL ONE DAY PURSUE YOU.

Instead of attempting to pursue boys, pursue Christ. I promise, there is nothing more exciting and adventurous than being completely en-thralled with the God who created you. Pursue Him. Chase after Him. Find your identity in Him alone. When you do this, one day a man who chases after Christ will pursue you—not the other way around.

2. PREPARE YOURSELF FOR MARRIAGE BY PURSUING THE MARKS OF WOMANHOOD.

I haven't written much on womanhood, but I know a lot of incredible, godly women who have. I would start with Elisabeth Elliot's amazing book, *Let Me Be a Woman*. Also, there are a ton of incredible resources at The Council on Biblical Manhood & Womanhood (cbmw.org).

KNOWING THE GOSPEL

Just like I stated above, begin by knowing the gospel. Don't just know it, though, know it enough to share it and teach it.

SACRIFICIAL HELPER

In Genesis 2:18, we see that God made woman as a helper for man. This does not mean women are lesser or weaker. Men and women are completely equal in dignity, value, and worth, but they are different in role and function. The role of being a helper is a characteristic of mature womanhood. Get around older women who can mentor and teach you how this plays out in the life of a biblical woman. One way you can do this now is by seeking the welfare of others around you—your home, friends, neighbors, fellow church members, etc. Practical ways women function as helpers are areas of decision-making, taking initiative in the home, and affirmation and encouragement, as well as a variety of other ways.

COURAGEOUS NURTURER

Nurturing reflects gentleness. The ways in which you can learn to nurture, even though you might not have children to nurture at this point in your life are numerous. You can nurture faith in yourself, and in your family and friends. You can learn to nurture health and emotional stability in yourself, and in your family and friends. Nurturing reflects one of the many roles of the Holy Spirit. Study the doctrine of the Holy Spirit and see how this role is magnified in mature womanhood. For a great resource on this, read Bruce Ware's powerhouse book, *Father, Son, and Holy Spirit.*

PROTECTOR OF TRUE BEAUTY

I use the word "protect" instead of "practice" here, because the definition of beauty is being changed and attacked in popular culture. Scan the front covers of magazines and listen to pop culture, and if you can stand it without throwing up, then you see an entirely different definition of beauty than what Scripture gives. In Christ, beauty becomes objective. It no longer is found in the "eye of the beholder." Pursue mature womanhood by protecting what is true beauty. God made you. You are fearfully and wonderfully made by Him. Rest in that. Believe that. Preach that. Practice that. Protect that.

GUARDING THE UNITY OF YOUR HOME

Another way you can practice this now is to learn to guard the unity of your home. Again, get around older women who model this and practice this. Hopefully you can find this in your relationship with your mom, but if not, get around older women. A woman who guards the unity of her home, instead of causing division or quarrels, is held in high esteem. This is the kind of stuff that is veiled in a post-Genesis 3 world, but seen as glorious in eternity.

3. INVITE OTHER LADIES INTO YOUR LIFE FOR **WISDOM** AND **ACCOUNTABILITY** (BOTH OLDER WOMEN AND PEERS).

Much like I said before, don't be a loan ranger. One of the biggest lies you can believe is that you don't need other people in your life. This is not Christianity. God created us to be in relationships with other people. God also created us to be mentored and discipled by others. This is a Titus 2 principle. Get older women around you for wisdom and accountability.

4. BE VOCAL ABOUT WHO YOU ARE IN CHRIST WHEN A MAN PURSUES YOU.

There is nothing more important than this. Before anything else, you are a daughter of the King. Be proud of that truth. Shout it from the mountaintops. Wear it on your sleeves. You are first and foremost a follower of the King of the universe. When you are pursued by someone, it shouldn't be a surprise for them to find out your first priority is your relationship with Christ. You don't have to wear cheesy, Christian t-shirts for people to know you are a Christian. Christ makes us different. If you are walking with Jesus, others will notice.

5. ALLOW YOUR DAD (OR CHRISTIAN COMMUNITY) TO BE YOUR LEADER, PROVIDER, AND PROTECTOR UNTIL THE DAY YOU GET MARRIED.

Until you are walked down the isle, your dad is your authority. If your dad isn't in your life, then the Christian community is your authority—other healthy male and female figures in your life. Don't believe the lie that you don't need anyone speaking into your life. Furthermore, don't believe the lie that it's none of your dad's business to be involved in your relationships. It's more than his business. It's his calling. Dads will stand before the King one day and give an account of how they shepherded and protected their daughters. Work together towards that end.

USE YOUR SINGLENESS FOR BIG AND RISKY THINGS

I have mentioned this several times already throughout this book, but I honestly think the riskiest thing you can do in this world is live courageously for Jesus. My good friend, Owen Strachan, says it this way,

> There are going to be moments in life, perhaps many, when it is not your circumstances that paralyze you. It is not physical or mental inability. It is not lack of capacity. No, what will stop you dead in your tracks is more simple.
>
> It will be a lack of boldness. It will be a failure to see the power of God, and to risk everything in this world to gain him.
>
> *Date Different* is a book that challenges you to be risky. I would like to think it's a book which focuses more on chasing after God and growing in holiness, then dating, sex, and marriage.[4]

Teenager and parent: be risky.

---

4 Strachan, Owen. *Risky Gospel: Abandon Fear and Build Something Awesome* (Nelson Books: Nashville, TN, 2013), 2.

Use your singleness for big and risky things. Follow Jesus. Date different. Serve in your local church. Volunteer in your local homeless shelter. Stand in front of an abortion clinic and plead with people to choose life. Go overseas during your summers and spring breaks. Use your singleness well.

THERE WILL BE A RISK

There is a price for redeeming our *view* and *practice* of dating, sex, and marriage, and I think one of the biggest prices to be paid in this endeavor is that **conflict** and **tension** are going to take place.

Conflict and tension are good things, though. Too often, we view conflict and tension in a negative light. We would rather live with a bunch of pink elephants in the room by sweeping stuff under the rug then have healthy conflict with other people. But again, conflict and tension, I think, are good things.

It is through conflict and tension that things change, real and authentic relationships begin to happen and go deeper, and movements begin to take place that change the world.

It is through conflict and tension that marriages are healed.

It was through conflict and tension that slavery was abolished.

It is through conflict and tension that the right to life is fought for.

And it is through conflict and tension that we change our *view* and **practice** of dating, sex, and marriage. This is how it will be redeemed. When you date different as young people, or you teach your children to date different, then you can be sure confrontation will loom its dreary head. Parents, if you haven't set a standard for dating from an early age, then you might find your teens rebelling against this new standard. Teenagers, if you choose to date and pursue marriage differently, then you will be met with opposition as well. Your peers might not understand at first. That guy or girl who likes you might be a little confused at first.

What do you mean you don't date as a sixteen-year-old?

What do you mean you are not only *saving* yourself for marriage but you are also *preparing* yourself for marriage?

If you choose this path for your life, you will be in some good company. People who have changed the world have not done so without much hardship.

And don't forget, it is through conflict and tension that Jesus saves us!

CHAPTER FOUR
GOD>ME>**THEM**>US>WE

THEM: Test the CHARACTER of the person you wish to date.

Several years ago, I was sitting in a coffee shop on my college campus and in walked this girl. I had been sitting at a table with a bunch of friends doing homework, as I first noticed her standing in line to purchase something. I knew who she was. We had talked a handful of times in the last few years. You could call us acquaintances at best.

For some reason, I knew I had to go over and talk to this girl. It was just one of those moments. You know what I'm talking about, right? The Lebron James hits a game winner in the corner and the crowd goes crazy type of moments? It was a moment like that for me. I remember every detail. What I was wearing. What she was wearing. Everything.

As the story goes, I get up out of my seat, and I walk over to her as she was standing in line waiting to purchase her item. We exchange greetings, and after a few minutes of small talk, I go back to my seat.

A few minutes of boldness... and my life was changed forever.

ATTRACTION OR CHARACTER?

When was the last time you looked across a room and noticed someone's character?[5] Never? Yeah, me either!

I looked across the room, and I noticed this girl immediately. She was beautiful. I'll just be honest. I was attracted to her. This girl's name is Grace, and she eventually became my wife. Having a wife is wayyyyyyyyyyyyyyyyy better than having a girlfriend by the way (just a side note). My point is simple, though. We usually base our "green lights" on physical attraction alone.

We often times jump into relationships because of physical attraction. We are attracted to this person, so we jump into the relationship without a season of getting to know them.

For this reason, I would argue the most important thing is not physical attraction, but character. And it takes awhile to get to know someone's character.

This chapter is about "them."

---

5 The following conversation on attraction and character needs to be referenced to Matt Chandler's book, *The Mingling of Souls*, 21-47.

GREEN LIGHTS AND RED LIGHTS

It takes time and intentionality to get to know someone, which is all the more reason to *date different*. If you jump into a relationship immediately, based on physical attraction, I think you are setting yourself up for failure.

Remember, this is a season to prepare, not a season to practice. As you prepare, take time to also get to know the character of the other person. Pay close attention to the green lights and red lights. If you see red lights, it may be wise not to enter this relationship. Often times, though, we can't get past our physical attractions. We suppress what's most important because we like what we see. That's why the process of **God Me Them Us We** is so important. Our relationship goes beyond just us. Here are some questions to help guide you during this season.

DO THEY HAVE A RELATIONSHIP WITH CHRIST?

This is the most important question for Christians in the history of dating. If you can't answer this with a green light, hold the breaks quick. Everything else flows from the answer to this question.

As far as evangelism dating, I'm glad you asked. I think it's one of the dumbest things ever. First of all, you aren't starting together on the same foundation. You are jumping into something that, I think, is potentially doomed from the beginning. Yes, I believe God is sovereign, but I also believe God gives us wisdom, and this is not wise. You will open up emotional attachments, potential physical attachments, and more. You might do more harm than good to the cause of Christ. God calls Christians to be equally yoked (2 Cor. 6:14). This means Christians should marry Christians. Therefore, if Jesus changes everything, then he changes everything, right? We don't just marry different, but we marry different.

ARE THEY INVOLVED IN THEIR LOCAL CHURCH?

After you get to know them on a spiritual level, get to know their involvement in their local church. It's easy to say you are a Christian, but do you see any fruit in the life of the other person? Watch their life as you get to know them. Are they serving in their local church? How committed are they to the Bride of Christ? What is more, involvement in a local church will prove their commitment to authority, as well as a growing relationship to Christ. As believers, we must walk under authority in every area of life (Rom. 13). As you get to know this person, watch how they respond to authority. This will be extremely important as the relationship progresses.

What is their reputation with others?

This is another important question. If they are known for being a turd, then you probably shouldn't date them. I'm not trying to be crude, but softer personalities often overcompensate to a personality completely different. Ask around. Get to know their friends. With whom are they spending time? Their reputation will tell you almost everything you need to know about their character. And remember, their character is the most important attribute.

WHAT IS THEIR FAMILY SITUATION LIKE?

How is her relationship with her dad? How is his relationship with his mom? The answers to these questions will tell you a lot. How a young man treats his mom and sisters will give you a glimpse into how he will treat you. How a young lady relates to her dad will give you a great example of how she will eventually relate to you. These aren't truisms, but they are important to know. They will give you wisdom and guide your potential relationship.

It's important to understand that her family becomes your family. Spend time watching how each family interacts with one another. You will spend much time together in the future. Remember, you are *leaving* and *cleaving* to a new family that God is allowing you to start.

DO YOU BELIEVE THE SAME THINGS ABOUT GOD?

Many couples fall short of diving into theological conversations before they begin their relationship. Again, for many, the most important thing is physical attraction. Part of getting to know the character of the person you potentially might date is getting to know their theological background. Here are some example questions you might explore together:

- Is the Bible the authority, infallible, and inspired Word of God?
- Does the Bible contain errors?
- What do you believe about the Trinity?
- What do you believe about the origin of the world?
- What is the role of the Church in a believer's life?
- What do you see as the role of the man within marriage?
- What do you see as the role of the woman within marriage?
- What do you believe about spiritual gifts?

- What do you believe about the relationship between God's sovereignty and human responsibility?

DO YOU HAVE THE SAME GOALS IN LIFE?

This is another key question to discuss together. Sometimes couples can be compatible in almost every way but this one. And this question is important. If the guy wants to be an accountant and stay close to dad and mom, and the girl wants to move to Africa and work with orphans, then I would think through whether or not this relationship might work—and then challenge the guy on his desire to stay close to dad and mom. This is a common obstacle for couples, and it's definitely not a deal breaker.

OTHER POTENTIAL CONVERSATIONS

1. GET TO KNOW THEIR TESTIMONY.

Talk through each person's testimony. A testimony is simply your life before Christ, your salvation story, and how your life is different now. Talk often about what God is doing in each of your lives.

2. IT'S NOT IMPORTANT TO TALK THROUGH EVERY DETAIL OF YOUR PAST SEXUAL EXPERIENCES.

I would recommend not talking through every detail of your past sexual escapades. I have found this more harmful than helpful for couples. If you haven't found yourself being pure through your teenage years, simply admit it. Leave out names, amount of times, and all details. Tell the other person you have repented and turned from those sins. Hopefully you are now walking in purity.

3. WHAT IS THE TIME FRAME FOR THIS RELATIONSHIP?

A final question to discuss is the time frame for this relationship before you get into it. It's important to begin relationships with a destination, and obviously there are only two final destinations for relationships—break up or get married.

As you hopefully get to know the character of the other person, and as you see this as a season to prepare and not practice dating, you will hopefully get to know this person well before you begin dating. I'm not talking about going through a "we're just talking" phase. That's a stupid thing to do.

This is an intentional season of becoming friends. Get to know one another. Enjoy one another's company. Begin to develop a relationship with one another's family. Talk about the Lord together. Attend your local church together, if you are able. Have fun. No pressure. Go to movies. Go out to eat. Have fun adventures together. The point is to be intentional during this time. If it doesn't work out, then it doesn't work out. God is still sovereign. He is still in control over you life. But seek to be above reproach in how you relate to one another. This is choosing to date different. This is courage. This is being counter-cultural.

Let's talk through the dating relationship now.

CHAPTER FIVE
GOD>ME>THEM>**US**>WE

US: Begin dating with marriage as the short-term end goal.

You may have already flipped here to read this chapter. I probably would have, too. If that's you, then go ahead and flip back to the beginning and start there. Don't get too excited now. This chapter won't make a lick of sense to you if you don't begin at the beginning. In fact, it might just make you mad. Well, it might make you mad anyways.

I want you to know that it's okay if this chapter makes you mad. Whenever I talk about early marriage, this is usually the content that makes people either want to break stuff or debate me.

As we begin this chapter, I want to remind you why this short book was written. My hope and prayer is that we (parents, student pastors, and teenagers) change the dating culture of young people within the Church. I don't think we should accept the way things are. I don't think we should reject it completely. *I think we should redeem it*. And that means several things have to change. Parents have to get serious about training their children for marriage, instead of just college. It means that parents enlist help, too. At my local church, that is why we place small group leaders in every child's life from the time they are two-years-old. We are promising parents they are not doing this crazy parenting thing alone.

It also means we challenge ourselves to go to war on sin... all sin. But before that conversation, let's remember the statistics we talked about in chapter one.

REMEMBER THE STATISTICS

FIRST STATISTIC: Nearly half (47%) of all high school students report having had sexual intercourse in 2011, a decline from 54% in 1991. Furthermore, males are slightly more likely than females to report having had sex (49% vs. 46%).

SECOND STATISTIC: 26% of female teens and 29% of male teens had more than one sexual partner in their lives. The percentage of high school students who report having had four or more sexual partners declined from 18% in 1995 to 15% in 2011.

THIRD STATISTIC: "Sexting" is the exchange of explicit sexual messages or images by someone's cell phone. 13% of 14–24 year olds report having shared a naked photo or video of themselves via digital communication such as the Internet or text messaging.[6]

STOP BLURRING THE LINES

It's safe to say the majority of teenagers are blurring the lines between dating, sex, and marriage. Our culture is so screwed up when it comes to gender identity, gender roles, dating, living together while dating, and redefining marriage, it comes as no surprise that teenagers are walking statistics of sexual failure.

Youth culture is often a reflection of the culture at large. And if parents aren't setting standards and raising the bar in their homes, then the Church has its work cut out for her. My prayer is that we would begin to see an army of teenagers get as passionate about sexual purity as they do about social justice issues.

I think it truly is that important.

THE INCREDIBLE DISCONNECT

Furthermore, we have created such an incredible disconnect between dating, sex, and marriage,

---

6 All 3 statistics come from the Kaiser Family Foundation (March 2013).

http://www.kff.org/womenshealth/upload/3040-06.pdf

that marriage has been delayed until later in life. Marriage is often delayed until well after college, while teens become hormonally active around 10-years-old—sometimes even earlier. This is one reason marriage was presented as a gift for young people all throughout history. They could pursue Christ, sexual holiness, and marriage as God opened the door for it.

As our sex-saturated culture continues to downplay the importance of marriage, we are going to continue to see an incredible disconnect between the pursuit of sexual holiness and biblical marriage.

As this takes place, and we delay marriage more and more, lust will dominate the lives of teenagers and twenty-somethings. If you struggle with lust, getting married is only the Band-Aid that covers up the true problem—a lack of holiness.

In 1 Thessalonians 4:1-8, Paul admonishes us, saying:

> Finally, then, brothers, we ask and urge you in the Lord Jesus, that as you received from us how you ought to walk and to please God, just as you are doing, that you do so more and more. 2 For you know what instructions we gave you through the Lord Jesus. 3 For this is the will of God, your sanctification: that you abstain from sexual immorality; 4 that each one of you know how to control his own body in holiness and honor, 5 not in the passion of

lust like the Gentiles who do not know God; **6** that no one transgress and wrong his brother in this matter, because the Lord is an avenger in all these things, as we told you beforehand and solemnly warned you. **7** For God has not called us for impurity, but in holiness. **8** Therefore whoever disregards this, disregards not man but God, who gives his Holy Spirit to you.

The Apostle Paul urges believers here to walk in a way that is pleasing to God—to run as fast as possible from sexual immorality. The will of God is that we abstain from sexual immorality and pursue the Lord Jesus Christ. As believers, God has called us to holiness and purity. As teenagers, God has called you to pursue holiness and purity, which is one reason I think getting married at an early age is a discussion the Church needs to be having.

WHY YOU SHOULD GET MARRIED AT AN EARLY AGE

Contrary to popular belief in today's culture, getting married young is still a good thing. It is an incredible thing. It is a noble thing. It is thing to be admired from the mountaintops.

Let me tell you why getting married at a young age is such a formidable joy. Let me note first, though, marriage is not necessarily a mark of *having arrived.* I know many men and women who practice manhood and womanhood at a high degree in their singleness.

Nonetheless, I digress...

1. IT PROVES OUR PURSUIT OF MATURE MANHOOD AND WOMANHOOD.

Much like how our works prove our faith (Jas. 2:17-18), the pursuit of adult things prove our desire to mature as men and women (1 Cor. 13:11). The opposite of being a child—or adolescent in our culture—is maturity. As men, we are called to pursue mature manhood, and likewise women in their pursuit of womanhood.

Mature manhood and womanhood are marked by the pursuit of mature things. That might seem redundant, but it can't be stated enough. The gospel beckons us all to intentional pursuits. After all, it is the fullness of Christ we are chasing after in our sanctification (Eph. 4:13). And marriage is a great discipline in our sanctification.

If we want to pursue maturity, then we have to practice consistency. And as a young person, the pursuit of marriage is a great mark of your pursuit of mature manhood and womanhood.

2. IT PROVES OUR DEPENDENCY ON GOD.

When my wife and I married, I had $15.00 in my bank account. You might call it an incredible act of faith. Some might call it being an idiot. That's okay. The reality, however, is that when we became married, we had to put an incredible amount of faith and dependency in God.

We weren't necessarily that young, either. I had just turned 23 by 8-days. My wife, Grace, was 22-years-old. We still had people attempting to speak into our lives, though, saying our ages were "too young" to get married.

A life marked by Christ is a full life of dependency. It's dependency in every aspect of life, including the pursuit of marriage at an early age.

3. IT PROVES WE ARE MERE HUMAN IN OUR SEXUALITY.

Think about this logically with me for a minute. Young people start having sexual desires around ten, eleven, or twelve years of age. At this point, even if they wait until the preferred "getting out of college age" that is still 10-or-so years of living with strong sexual desires. That is one reason why marriage throughout history was much earlier.

In 1 Corinthians 7:8-9, Paul says, "But I say to the unmarried and to widows that it is good for them if they remain even as I. But if they do not have self-control, let them marry; for it is better to marry than to burn with passion..."

According to Paul, a lack of self-control is actually one reason to get married, and I would argue that it is also one reason, in our culture, to get married at an early age.

4. IT PROVES OUR DESIRE TO STAND AGAINST THE TIDE.

I don't have to convince you that the biblical foundation of marriage is under attack in our culture. Part of what it means to flourish as men and women is to embrace the roles God has created for us.

Men and women are absolutely equal in dignity, value, and worth, but we are different in role and function. This means we operate differently—biologically, physically, emotionally, and functionally.

When you as a young person embrace the pursuit of early marriage, you are standing firm on the Word of God by embracing the roles God has designed for you at an early age. By doing this, you are reflecting back to the world not only God's design for gender roles, but also God's design for marriage.

Your lifestyle then becomes the finest, Christ-centered apologetic to your closest family, friends, and neighbors (Jude 1).

5. IT PROVES THAT GOD'S DESIGN FOR MARRIAGE IS NOT A CULTURAL BENCHMARK FOR YOUR LIFE.

So many of us have the pursuit of marriage backwards. We tend to think of the pursuit of marriage after these other cultural things happen in our life: go off to college, graduate college, get internships, get a master's degree, get a nice paying job, buy a house, have a 401(k), etc.

Only after all of these things are complete are we able to pursue marriage. This view puts marriage as just another thing to check off on your list of cultural benchmarks to accomplish in your life. Marriage, however, is quite the opposite.

Marriage is the oldest institution in history. It was in the Garden of Eden that God instituted marriage between one woman and one man (Gen. 2:24). It was a foreshadow of the greatest institution to come centuries later.

What is more, Paul doesn't call marriage a game, a sinking ship, an anchor in someone's life, or a thorn. No! He calls it a reflection of a great mystery (Eph. 5:32)—the mystery between Christ and his Bride.

And it's still a good thing for you. Let's move our conversation now towards sex and purity.

IF YOU CANNOT EXERCISE SELF-CONTROL

As I mentioned above, in 1 Corinthians 7:6-9, Paul says this:

> Now as a concession, not a command, I say this. 7 I wish that all were as I myself am. But each has his own gift from God, one of one kind and one of another.
>
> 8 To the unmarried and the widows I say that it is good for them to remain single as I am. 9 **But if they cannot exercise self-control, they should marry.** For it is better to marry than to burn with passion.

Do you see what the Apostle Paul is saying here? As advice, and a command, he is urging those who cannot exercise self-control to be married. This should be our first talking point as parents, student pastors, and teenagers. Are you currently struggling with sexual desire? If yes, then it's time to begin preparing for marriage. It's foolish to struggle with sexual desire and then delay marriage until later in life.

As I have mentioned above, I don't think getting married means you have arrived. There could be one million reasons in which someone is not married later in life. Again, use your singleness well. Use it for big things. Go to far places. Do hard things. Be courageous in your singleness.

However, if able, I do think it's wise to pursue marriage earlier in life.

EVERYTHING YOU DO IS WORSHIP

Let's start in Romans 12:1-2. It reads:

> I appeal to you therefore, brothers, by the mercies of God, to present your bodies as a living sacrifice, holy and acceptable to God, which is your spiritual worship. 2 Do not be conformed to this world, but be transformed by the renewal of your mind, that by testing you may discern what is the will of God, what is good and acceptable and perfect.

There is a lot of weight to this topic. How you handle sex within your teenage years can potentially crush you, or it potentially will lead you to prosper. My prayer for you is that you would chase after King Jesus as hard as you possibly can. Live life courageously. Live life honorably. Live life with a posture of holiness.

According to Romans 12, worship is not just singing songs and getting emotional; it's presenting your body as a living sacrifice—meaning everything you do is worship.

You can't live this way if you don't know Jesus. So, if you're reading this book, then you're going to think what I'm about to say is goofy and stupid. And if you're a believer in Jesus—and you think what I'm about to say is goofy and stupid—then that should scare you to death, because there is no room for a sinful approach to sex in a believer's life.

THE TENSION OF BEHAVIOR MODIFICATION

My goal in this entire discussion is not to modify your behavior, or scare you into some sort of good behavior. That's what some of you do as parents. It's called behavior modification parenting. You attempt to modify your child's behavior in how you reward them for their good behavior. This type of parenting voids the actual heart issues taking place within your child. It fails, because it doesn't get to the root. That's what I don't want you to feel as you read these pages.

In my house, we are trying our best to teach my daughter that good behavior flows from a happy heart rooted in Jesus, not from a desire to get candy and donuts as her reward. So, every evening when I arrive home from work, my kids run to greet me at the door; we've made it a game. As the kids run towards me, I dodge, dip, duck, dive, and dodge out of the way, so I can hug and kiss Grace first. She is number one. I then get down on my knees and ask my daughter about her day. Every single day, she is working to have a "good report with her mama and her brother" that she can tell her daddy.

Here's the deal, though, I'm not giving her money when she has a good report. I hug her, kiss her, and remind her that God wants us to have happy hearts because he already loves us, and he proved it when Jesus was crucified. She doesn't have to earn daddy's love or God's love.

Do you get it? I don't want to modify your behavior. Or scare you. My prayer is that God would get a hold of your heart, and he would change you from the inside out. My prayer is that you would use your bodies as living sacrifices, not instruments of immorality.

GOD, GROSS, OR GIFT?[7]

Sex can be viewed in one of three ways. It can be viewed as god, gross, or gift. The first two ways are pure idolatry. Idolatry is putting something or someone in the place of your worship of God. It's placing someone or something into a god-like status.

---

7 The conversation following on sex as either god, gross, or gift was highly referenced from works on The Resurgence website that no longer exists. Research was done prior to its ending.

SEX CAN BE A <u>GOD</u> IN YOUR LIFE

In our culture, this is often the main view of sex. Watch any television show, movie, listen to mainstream music, etc., and you will see a culture that elevates sex. Remember, culture flows downstream, but sin is rampant everywhere.

For our purposes in this discussion, it's probably viewed as god in these ways:

- Watching pornography (which generates revenues of $90 billion worldwide).
- Sending pictures of yourself that you shouldn't be sending to others... ever!
- And sinful relationships in which you might be in right now.

The first commandment commands us to worship God alone. If we obey this command, then we don't find ourselves worshipping other people and other things (like sex) as functional gods. If we find ourselves falling into sin, we still continue to worship, but do so as idolaters treating people and things as gods. Do you see the point? Sometimes sex can be our god. We disobey God, stop worshipping him, and start worship things and people.

Sexual sin is idolatry. I have heard it said many times that idolatry happens when a good thing (like sex) becomes a god thing (like watching pornography). Idolatry begins in the heart.

Someone or something becomes the center of our lives. Again, this is idolatry. If we don't have that person, or that thing, then we become miserable. When this type of posture towards sex takes place, sex becomes a god in your life.

Again, in Romans 12:1, Paul flat out states that worship is offering our bodies to God as a living sacrifice.

In 1 Corinthians 10:7-8, Paul makes this connection between sexual sin and idolatry, saying, "Do not become idolaters as were some of them... nor let us commit sexual immorality, as some of them did."

In Romans 1:24-25, Paul wrote that people either worship God as Creator and enjoy His creation—including our bodies—or people worship creation as a god, and in sexual sin offer their bodies in worship to others.

God gave them up in the lusts of their hearts to impurity, to the dishonoring of their bodies among themselves, **25** because they exchanged the truth about God for a lie and worshiped and served the creature rather than the Creator.

Paul went onto explain those who worship creation invariably worship the human body and its pleasure through sinful sex—including homosexuality—because it is the apex of God's creation.

LET ME TALK ABOUT PORNOGRAPHY FOR A SECOND

Pornography is killing us.

The porn business makes several billion dollars worldwide each year. That makes me want to punch something... as hard as I possibly can.

Everyday 2.5 million pornographic emails are sent.

Most recent statistics tell us that 90 percent of children between the ages of eight and sixteen have viewed pornography on the Internet.

The average age of first Internet exposure to pornography is eleven.

The largest consumer of Internet pornography is boys ages 12-17.[8]

If you are struggling with looking at pornography—it doesn't matter if you are a young man or young woman—I would encourage you to do whatever it takes to go to war on this in your life. Get rid of your computers, tablets, and smartphones. But most importantly, confess this sin, both to God and to someone else. The first step to overcoming an addiction is confession that you have one.

Also, it would be good to get a filter for your devices. Covenant Eyes would be my recommen-

---

8 For more statistics, visit covenanteyes.com.

dation. As parents, it allows you to have absolute control over what your children are viewing on their devices.

SEX CAN BE A <u>GROSS</u> THING IN YOUR LIFE

There are a few ways sex can be seen as gross. They are most commonly seen in these ways:

The first way sex could potentially be seen as gross in your life is if you have experienced bad teaching on sex. Bad teaching on sex leads to a bad understanding of sex. These teachings might say something like, "Don't have sex, because you don't want to be all *used up* for your future spouse." That is a horrendous way to look at it and teach it.

The second way, for our discussion here, might be that you've had bad experiences with sex. I'm talking about the terrible acts of molestation or rape. This is a reality for many people. If this terrible act of sin has happened to you, then you might have a bad view of sex at this point in your life. I would encourage you to confess this to someone immediately. This is something you will need to work through with a counselor for a heavy season of your life.

Finally, you might see sex as gross if you are embarrassed by it. We should never be embarrassed by sex, because sex is a gift given by God to us. God created it. Within the appropriate context (marriage), we are to enjoy this great gift God has given us.

SEX SHOULD BE SEEN AS A <u>GIFT</u> IN YOUR LIFE

Sex should never be elevated to god-like status in your life, and it should never be viewed as gross either. It should absolutely be viewed as a gift.

I mentioned in chapter 2 that we should never awaken love until two becomes one. In other words, sex should be seen as a gift in the right context. Without the context of marriage, sex is a sin.

SEX< >CONTEXT

You might say it this way—*sex* and *context* need each other. Without both of these things together, it is sin. And again, it will crush you!

PRIMARY REASONS FOR SEX

I would submit to you that God primarily gives the gift of sex for 3 reasons.

1. SEX IS FOR PLEASURE.

Read the entire book of Song of Solomon. It is all about the pleasures of sex within the right context.

2. SEX IS FOR PROCREATION —OR CREATING CHILDREN.

Genesis 1:28 says, "Be fruitful and multiple and fill the earth and subdue it." This is the first command God gives to Adam and Eve in the Garden of Eden. The gift of children is a result of sex within marriage.

3. SEX IS FOR ONENESS.

Genesis 1:24-25 (one of my favorite verses in all of Scripture) says, "Therefore a man shall leave his father and his mother and hold fast to his wife, and they shall become **one flesh**. And **the man** and **his wife** were **both naked** and were **not ashamed**."

MARRIAGE IS THE CONTEXT FOR SEX

Sex is a GIFT within the context of marriage, given by God, to married couples. Sex is not given as a gift to boyfriends and girlfriends. It's not given as a gift to middle schoolers or high schoolers. It's not given as a gift to couples who are engaged. Sex is a gift given by God to be pursued without fear, without hesitation, in full safety, in full unity, and in the full covenant commitment of marriage alone!

Anything outside of that—whether pornography, sending inappropriate pictures of yourself, a relationship you are in that you shouldn't be in, or anything, God forbid, that has happened to you sexually in a terrible way—is an absolute abomination and spit in the face of the God who created sex and perfectly gave it to us to be enjoyed in the context of marriage. May you date different. May you see the beauty of God in your relationships.

IF YOU AREN'T A CHRISTIAN YET...

First of all, I would encourage you to repent of your sin and believe in the gospel. Go back to chapter two for a clear presentation of what the gospel is and how to respond to it.

You don't have to work to "be good," because Jesus "was good" for you.

You can't view sex as a gift if you don't believe in the Giver of that gift.

YOU ARE NEVER TOO DIRTY OR USED UP FOR GOD

Some of you may be sitting there reading this and feel like it's too late for you, because you've already messed up. You might feel dirty. You might feel used up. You might feel like no one could ever want you anymore if they knew the things you have done.

You might feel like God couldn't love you anymore because of the things you have done.

Here's what you need to hear right now: **God loves you! You don't have to earn his love.** You don't have to earn his love no matter how far you run from him. He is still pursuing you, and he is waiting for you to return home with arms opened wide.

WHAT'S NEXT?

Here is some application for you as we end this chapter.

1. DON'T BE A FOOL!

Proverbs 12:15 says, "The way of a fool is right in his own eyes, but a wise man listens to advice." Proverbs 14:12 says, "There is a way that seems right to a man, but its end is the way to death."

2. RESPOND TO GOD!

Respond to God in worship. God created you and gave you a shape and purpose, and he has a perfect plan for your life. How do we know this? Well, because God creates all things. He has created you, and he, too, has created a plan for your life. What God creates is good. Furthermore, respond in worship because God gives us incredible gifts—like sex—to be used in the proper context.

3. REPENT!

Repent if you are in a relationship in which you shouldn't be. Repent if you are looking at pornography. Repent if you are treating your brothers and sisters in Christ as objects.

Young men, you should treat your sisters in Christ like **treasures to protect** instead of **objects to be used**.

When you live this way, it brings the most formidable of joys, because this is how you were created to live.

4. GET TO KNOW ONE ANOTHER BY MOVING YOUR RELATIONSHIP ALONG IN A HEALTHY WAY.

Let's talk about that now.

CHAPTER SIX
GOD>ME>THEM>US>**WE**

WE: Involve your parents (and the faith community) in your relationship for wisdom and accountability as you move forward.

You might be asking at this point, "What is the difference between *us* and *we*?" The difference is found in *who* is involved. Let's list it out this way, for clarity:

GOD: In all things, begin with God and his design for it.

ME: This is a season to prepare, not a season to practice.

THEM: Test the CHARACTER of the person you wish to date.

US: Begin dating with marriage as the short-term end goal.

WE: Involve your parents (and the faith community) in your relationship for wisdom and accountability as you move forward.

Begin with God. Prepare yourself for marriage. Move toward testing the character of the person you wish to date. Begin dating with marriage as the short-term end goal, practicing the guardrails you have in place for purity. Finally, involve others in your relationship for wisdom and accountability. This is dating different. Teenagers, this is courageous dating. Parents, this is courageous parenting.

SIDE BAR FOR THE GUYS

Here is some encouragement. I want to raise the bar for young men in the Church today. I want to see an army of young men be counter-cultural in their dating. When you are ready to pursue a young woman for marriage, before you even ask her out on a date, you need get permission from her dad to even date her. Listen, I'm not even talking marriage yet.

What would it look like if you were so wrapped up in your pursuit of Jesus that you wanted to do everything right? At this point, you are ready for marriage. You are ready to pursue the person you have been getting to know. What if you actually set up a breakfast meeting with her dad and laid out your intentions in pursuing his daughter? And then you actually asked his permission if you could pursue her? Say huh? That is a fourth-quarter-games-on-the-line-type-of-awesome. I want to see more dudes with that type of intentionality.

Here's why this is important. Until a dad walks his daughter down the isle and gives her away on her marriage day, the dad is the leader, provider, and protector of his little girl. Not you, bro! Even in your dating relationship, and even in your engagement, you are number two. Her dad is her leader, provider, and protector. What if her dad is not involved, though? If her dad isn't involved spiritually, then you still honor him. It would speak volumes if you still asked his permission and asked for him to walk with you all through this process. That is mountain shaking stuff right there. Who's ready for that challenge?

HAVE YOU MADE YOUR INTENTIONS CLEAR TO YOUR PARENTS, AND TO OTHER BELIEVERS IN YOUR LIFE?

This is the most important question as you move forward into a relationship. Have you made your intentions clear to your parents and to other believers in your life? If not, do this right now. Set up a meeting tomorrow. Take them to dinner tonight. Also, do you have approval by godly (and older) counsel?

Make your intentions known to other believers in your life, as well. This is Titus 2 discipleship. Titus 2:2-10 reads:

> Older men are to be sober-minded, dignified, self-controlled, sound in faith, in love, and in

steadfastness. **3** Older women likewise are to be reverent in behavior, not slanderers or slaves to much wine. They are to teach what is good, **4** and so train the young women to love their husbands and children, **5** to be self-controlled, pure, working at home, kind, and submissive to their own husbands, that the word of God may not be reviled.

6 Likewise, urge the younger men to be self-controlled. **7** Show yourself in all respects to be a model of good works, and in your teaching show integrity, dignity, **8** and sound speech that cannot be condemned, so that an opponent may be put to shame, having nothing evil to say about us. **9** Bondservants are to be submissive to their own masters in everything; they are to be well-pleasing, not argumentative, **10** not pilfering, but showing all good faith, so that in everything they may adorn the doctrine of God our Savior.

Older men and older women are to pass down the truths of the faith to the next generation. Dating different means getting around older men and older women who will walk with you through this process.

INVOLVE PARENTS IN YOUR RELATIONSHIP

As parents, you should be involved in almost every detail of your teenager's relationship until they reach marriage. Some might call this legalism or helicopter parenting. I would disagree with that notion. I think it's good leadership, good stewardship, and good parenting.

You will one day stand before God and give an account for your parenting. Work as hard as you can to point your children toward purity. In fact, you are the guardians of their purity. How you talk with them about dating, sex, and marriage will set the tone for how they view those things, as well.

What does this look like practically? Well, I think it could look different for every set of parents and teenagers, depending on their maturity level. But here's the deal, I wouldn't trust a hormonally charged teenage boy for 3-seconds in a room alone with my daughter. With that said, there are some things that transcend all families. Here are some steps to take:

- Meet with the other set of parents and get to know them. Spend time with them often.
- Set up a weekly or bi-weekly meeting with the couple for accountability and teaching moments.
- If you're a dad, ask your sons the hard questions. Make honesty and openness a part of the rhythms of your home.
- Set boundaries for the couple. It's not because you don't trust them; it's because... well, you don't trust them. Who would? We are all fallen sinners working out of

our redemption in Christ. But we are still sinners.
* Work with them toward the short-term end goal of marriage.

INVOLVE THE FAITH COMMUNITY IN YOUR RELATIONSHIP

Work toward involving the faith community—the Church—in your relationship as best as you can, as well. I have seen couples all too often become secluded in their relationship. They spend too much time alone, and eventually begin to marginalize and even lose friends.

Spend the majority of your time with other people and with other couples. Limit your alone time. And just a rule of thumb that has nothing to do with this section, never ever have horizontal couch time. Horizontal couch time just leads to bad things. Stay far away from horizontal couch time.

The more you can involve your brothers and sisters in Christ in your relationship, the healthier it will be.

QUESTIONS TO ASK IF YOU'RE IN A DATING RELATIONSHIP

If you can't answer "YES" to each of these questions, then I encourage you to push the pause button on your relationship until the two of you figure some things out together.

1. ARE WE STAYING PURE?

If you aren't staying pure, it's either time to get married or end things. I'm not trying to be crude, but if Grace and I had decided to make our engagement longer, I don't know if I would've been able to control myself. If you're the type of guy who is like, "Oh, but I'm not like you; I can control myself," then you're a lying idiot.

2. ARE WE INVOLVING OTHERS IN OUR 'DATING RELATIONSHIP' FOR **WISDOM** AND ACCOUNTABILITY?

As mentioned above, this is important for wisdom and accountability. You don't want to be lone rangers in your relationship. Get other, godly people around you. Get mentors around you. Get brothers and sisters around you to hold you accountable.

3. WHO IS HOLDING US ACCOUNTABLE AND ASKING US THE HARD QUESTIONS?

Now that you agree with me, who are the people actually holding you accountable and asking you the hard questions? Make a list. Go talk to them today. Ask them to be praying for your relationship often.

4. DO WE HAVE THE FUTURE IN MIND?

Hopefully by now you understand my viewpoint on dating, sex, and marriage. I think dating should be intentional and short. Are you talking about the future often?

5. ARE WE **BOTH** READY FOR MARRIAGE?

This is an important question. All too often, I see one person in the relationship ready for marriage, but the other person isn't. They want to travel the world for a season, or get 15 degrees to put on their wall before they get marriage. If you both aren't ready for marriage, then you might have something to work through before you move forward.

6. WHAT IS OUR PLAN TO GET THERE?

Do you have plan? If you're plan is to date for 3-years, get 2 degrees, and have a 1.5 year long engagement, then it's a pretty terrible plan. I would suggest that you know pretty soon if you could marry the other person. With intentionality, I think you know within 4 to 6-months if marriage is a reality for your relationship. Talk through a plan. Make it short. Get other people involved. Seek out wisdom. Don't delay.

AND, FINALLY, KEEP YOUR ENGAGEMENTS SHORT AND DON'T ACT LIKE YOU'RE MARRIED WHEN YOU'RE NOT

Do not awaken love until 2 becomes 1. Okay, you get that by now. But how does this play out practically for a dating couple?

I think it's important to set standards and operate within that framework all through your dating season. Most of the time, the conversation involves only sexual safeguards, but I think you should have conversations concerning emotional and spiritual safeguards, as well.

Here are some principles to live by to not act like your married when your not:

- Don't use the words "I love you" until you are engaged. Honor each other by protecting one another emotionally.
- Guard one another spiritually by not having devotions together until you are en-

gaged or married. You are not her spiritual leader, bro. Her dad is. If he isn't involved, then the faith community is.

- Pray for each other, not with each other. People might disagree with me on this one, but I think it's important to not open the door of spiritual intimacy until 2 becomes 1. Spiritual intimacy leads to emotional intimacy, which leads to physical intimacy, which leads to repentance.
- Guard your time alone. Don't act like a married couple relationally when you're not. Be above reproach in public and in private. Remember, how you act in public will often be heightened in private, and people will see right through it.

Keep your dating time short.

Keep your engagement time short.

Love Jesus the most. Be courageous. Be bold. Be different. Be counter-cultural.

Remember, Jesus changes everything—even how we date.

Now go and date different and change the world.

APPENDIX ONE
ENCOURAGEMENT FOR DADS OF YOUNG DAUGHTERS

1. DATE THEM NOW AND OFTEN.

If you don't have a weekly—or a few times a month—daddy date with your daughters, then get that going immediately.

2. SET THE BAR HIGH.

Set the bar high for any dude who tries to pursue your daughter. Date them and treat them like royalty. When it's time for them to be pursued, the bar will be right where it needs to be.

3. SET A CLEAR STANDARD IN YOUR HOME FROM AN EARLY AGE.

Talk with your daughters at an early age about what your home will look like with friends and boys. I am under the personal rule that you shouldn't date until you are ready for marriage. Preach it from an early age. But remember, you are the one who is dating them during this time.

4. HAVE A PURITY WEEKEND BETWEEN MOM AND DAUGHTER WHEN ENTERING 6TH GRADE.

When entering 6th grade, have a purity weekend where mom and daughter go away and have a special weekend together. During this weekend, begin the conversation on dating, sex, and marriage. Challenge and parent them to *date different*.

APPENDIX TWO
ENCOURAGEMENT FOR DADS OF YOUNG SONS

1. SPEND RELATIONAL TIME WITH THEM OFTEN.

Spend as much relational time with your son as possible. Take them to ball games. Go hunting together. Go to movies. Go out to eat. Just spend time with your son—both quality and quantity time.

2. ENGAGE THEM SPIRITUALLY AND EMOTIONALLY.

Throughout their young childhood, engage your son both spiritually and emotionally. Let them see you model your faith. Part of modeling your faith will be modeling repentance. Begin to talk with them about deep things. Pray with them. Let them see your passion for your King.

3. TEACH THEM BIBLICAL MANHOOD AT AN EARLY AGE.

Dads, it is your job to teach your son the marks of mature manhood. Read books with them. Memorize Scripture with them. Help them learn to be leaders, providers, and protectors at an early age. This is your most important aim as a dad.

4. HAVE A PURITY WEEKEND BETWEEN DAD AND SON WHEN ENTERING 6TH GRADE.

When ready, take your sons on a purity weekend. Do something awesome together. Go and kill stuff. During this weekend, begin the conversation on dating, sex, and marriage. Challenge and parent them to *date different*.

DATE DIFFERENT GRAPHIC

HOW TO DATE
DIFFERENT

FOR THE GUYS

Don't pursue girls, pursue Christ, then pursue a woman.

Prepare yourself for manhood by pursuing the marks of manhood:
- KNOWING the gospel
- SACRIFICIAL Leadership
- HARD Work
- Protecting Women at ALL COSTS
- Making good decisions for the benefit of OTHERS

Invite other dudes into your life for wisdom and accountability.

Pursue a girl with her dad's approval, but don't date until you are ready for marriage.

FOR THE GIRLS

Don't pursue boys, pursue Christ & a man one day will pursue you.

Prepare yourself for marriage by pursuing the marks of womanhood:
- KNOWING the gospel
- SACRIFICIAL Helper
- COURAGEOUS Nurturer
- Protector of TRUE Beauty
- Guarding the UNITY of Your Home

continued on back

HOW TO DATE
DIFFERENT

FOR THE GIRLS
CONT.

Invite other ladies into your life for wisdom and accountability.

Be vocal about who you are in Christ when a man pursues you.

Allow your dad (or Christian community) to be your leader, provider, and protector until the day you are married.

FOR THE COUPLE

Ask yourself the hard questions:

-Are both of our parents involed?
-Are we both ready for marriage?
-Are we staying pure?
-Are we involving others in our 'dating relationship' for wisdom and accountability?

Have we made our intentions clear to each other, to our parents, and to other believers in our life?

What is our time frame for marriage?

What is our plan to get there?

Who is holding us accountable?

HOW TO DATE DIFFERENT
SUMMARY:
<GOD, ME, THEM, US, WE>

GOD	In all things, begin with God and his design for it.
ME	This is a season to prepare, not a season to practice.
THEM	Test the CHARACTER of the person you wish to date.
US	Begin dating with marriage as the short-term end goal.
WE	Involve your parents (and the faith community) in your relationship for wisdom and accountability as you move forward.

ABOUT THE AUTHOR

Founder of Veritas, Greg serves as an executive elder and the family ministries pastor at Foothills Church in Knoxville, TN, overseeing the crib through college life-stage teams.

Greg also serves as the Executive Editor and Communications Director for The Council on Biblical Manhood & Womanhood (CBMW), a leading conservative evangelical think tank on gender, marriage, and sexuality.

Greg speaks all over the country at youth and college conferences, disciple-now weekends, men's conferences, family conferences, and more. He is the author of *Reformational Manhood: Creating a Culture of Gospel-Centered Warriors*, *Date Different: A Short (but honest) Conversation on Dating, Sex & Marriage for Teenagers (and their parents)*, and *50 Truths to Teach Your Preschooler about God*.

He received a M.Div. in Biblical and Theological Studies from SBTS and a B.A. in Biblical Studies from Boyce College.

He resides in Knoxville, TN with his wife, Grace, and their two children.

CONNECT WITH GREG:

VERITAS: theveritasnetwork.org
TWITTER: @greggibson86
CBMW: cbmw.org

Made in the USA
Lexington, KY
18 June 2016